Cape Cod
on my mind

A. BLAKE GARDNER

" *Perhaps the greatest gift of the Cape is the intimacy we have with sky and sea and shining sands.* "

Gladys Taber

FALCON®

The tide infiltrates Eastham's Nauset Marsh, part of the popular Cape Cod National Seashore. PAUL REZENDES

Age by age, the sea here gives battle to the land; age by age, the earth struggles for her own, calling to her defence her energies and her creations, bidding her plants steal down upon the beach, and holding the frontier sands in a net of grass and roots which the storms wash free.

Henry Beston

3

A monument commemorating the Pilgrim's first landing in the New World overlooks the fishing fleet in Provincetown Harbor. PAUL REZENDES

Candy-striped Sankaty Lighthouse commands a panoramic view of both land and sea from a 90-foot bluff on Nantucket Island. PAUL REZENDES

Community support rebuilt 1,350-foot-long Sandwich Boardwalk after Hurricane Bob destroyed it in 1991. JEFF GREENBERG

66 The beach is a vast beatitude, that brings light to the dark corners of a man's heart. 99

Henry C. Kittredge

The sun sets fire to an abandoned whelk shell. ALISON SHAW

A new day at Coast Guard Beach in Eastham promises tranquility. A. BLAKE GARDNER

Scallops of surf skirt the wide expanse of Cisco Beach on Nantucket Island. PAUL REZENDES

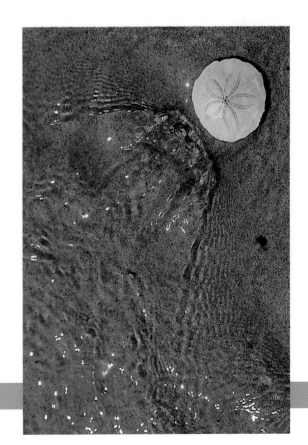

The Atlantic grabs greedily for a sand dollar.
FREDERICK D. ATWOOD

A perfect day on Marconi Beach never seems to last long enough. SUSAN COLE KELLY

A castle construction crew breaks ground on Marconi Beach. KINDRA CLINEFF

Warm sand and welcome bouts of shade make up the *fun*-damentals of a summer playground. STEPHEN TRIMBLE

66 Cool breath of eastern ocean, the aroma of beach vegetation in the sun, the hot, pungent exhalation of fine sand—these mingled are the midsummer savour of the beach. 99

Henry Beston

> *Nantucket is... almost part and parcel of the ocean; as much in league with the waters as Venice, its very buildings seasoned with tar and the salt winds.*

James Morris

A sea gull tests his "land legs."
DAVID G. CURRAN

The weathered, shingled cottages of Nantucket are the quintessential background for boats idling in port. PAUL REZENDES

13

Elaborate Victorian houses embellish the streets of Oak Bluffs on Martha's Vineyard. LOU PALMIERI / NEW ENGLAND STOCK PHOTO

" *May on Cape Cod is the year at its gayest. There is a passion of blooming.* "

Gladys Taber

A child's spray brightens a day at Farmer's Market.
ALISON SHAW

Delicately carved wedding-cake trim turns an Oak Bluffs cottage into a gingerbread house. PAUL REZENDES

A Greek Revival sea captain's home is a stately reminder of the days when Edgartown was a prosperous whaling port. PAUL REZENDES

Who wouldn't want to wander down the garden path of this charming Edgartown home? ALISON SHAW

An arbor opens into the secluded garden of a French restaurant in Siasconset.
THOMAS P. BENINCAS JR. / NEW ENGLAND STOCK PHOTO

Quaint cobblestone streets are one hallmark of the importance that Nantucket Town places on historical preservation. PAUL REZENDES

*"*All houses on Cape Cod are at least two hundred and fifty years old, and about one third of them are the oldest house in town.*"*

Clair Baisly

A lamppost dated 1885 marks Lieutenant Max Wagner Square in Nantucket Town. DAVID WEINTRAUB

Leaded-glass windows hint at the age of the Jethro Coffin House, built in 1686 and billed as the oldest house on Nantucket. PAUL REZENDES

Swamp maple leaves react to dropping temperatures and dwindling daylight at Higgins Pond in Nickerson State Park. A. BLAKE GARDNER

Autumn ignites the Old Beech Stand at the Cape Cod Museum of Natural History in Brewster. PAUL REZENDES

Robins are common throughout the Cape in spring and fall. FREDERICK D. ATWOOD

Like the pounding Atlantic surf, winter leaves its mark on Coast Guard Beach. A. BLAKE GARDNER

" The face of the sea is always changing. Crossed by colors, lights, and moving shadows, sparkling in the sun, mysterious in the twilight, its aspects and its moods vary hour by hour. The surface waters move with the tides, stir to the breath of the winds, and rise and fall to the endless, hurrying forms of the waves. "

Rachel Carson

Built in 1873, Stoney Brook Grist Mill is a picturesque memento of the many mills that have operated near Brewster over the centuries. SUSAN COLE KELLY

A Dutch windmill graces the grounds of the Aptucxet Trading Post, birthplace of commerce in the New World. DAVID G. CURRAN

A Cataumet farmer finds that a single-horsepower antique plow is enough to clear a snow-clogged road. DAVID G. CURRAN

A layer of frosting makes everything more palatable. FREDERICK D. ATWOOD

Hoarfrost turns an evergreen into a breathtaking work of art. FREDERICK D. ATWOOD

Locked in brittle beauty by a wash of winter cobalt, Wood End Lighthouse helps guide
sea captains around the tip of the Cape.   A. BLAKE GARDNER

Technicolor buoys overrun the wall of a home near Red Brook Harbor. DAVID G. CURRAN

> ❝ *The Cape Codder's feeling for nature is bone-deep and is especially endearing. Living with the sea around them has much to do with it, I think.* ❞
>
> Gladys Taber

A lobster fisherman brandishes dinner for two.
KINDRA CLINEFF

Commercial fishing boats have lined the wharves in Provincetown since
before the town was incorporated in 1727.   JEFF GNASS

A long day's work pays off for this "old salt."
STEVEN MORELLO

Careful management and an eye to conservation suggest a promising future for striped bass fishing, both sport and commercial. KINDRA CLINEFF

" There is a certain mystique about the striped bass. They are the fisherman's enigma, the muse of these cold waters. Stripers seem to come by magic, to an individual call, prompting superstitious thinking. Stripers drive fishermen crazy. "

Cynthia Huntington

Within this 1857 oyster shack, the Bayside Lobster Hutt serves up "lobster in the rough." DAVID WEINTRAUB

Open-air cafés abound in Provincetown, many offering fresh fish straight from the docks. SUSAN COLE KELLY

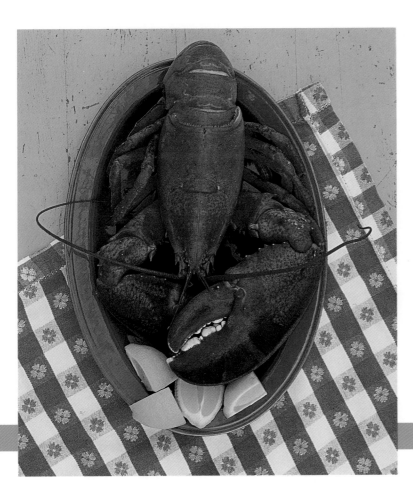

A Cape café serves up its blue-plate special. ALISON SHAW

Band concerts, fireworks, and starry summer nights attract throngs of visitors to Ocean Park in Oak Bluffs.   ALISON SHAW

The local militia salutes Independence Day on the village green in Falmouth, one of the few Cape towns attacked by the British during the Revolution.   DAVID G. CURRAN

The Cape Cod Baseball League delivers fine family entertainment, in this case at Coady Field in Bourne.   DAVID G. CURRAN

"A rainy day is the perfect time for a walk in the woods.... Then all the needles on the evergreens wear a sheath of silver; ferns seem to have grown to almost tropical lushness and every leaf has its edging of crystal drops. Strangely colored fungi—mustard-yellow and apricot and scarlet—are pushing out of the leaf mold and all the lichens and mosses have come alive with green and silver freshness."

Rachel Carson

A mushroom takes center stage in a sphagnum bog. FREDERICK D. ATWOOD

A boardwalk slices through Atlantic White Cedar Swamp over peat bogs up to 7 feet deep. LAURENCE PARENT

Spiders weave a wispy veil beneath the delicate blossoms of the pipsissewa. FREDERICK D. ATWOOD

" Every turn of the road, every green plot and half-hidden avenue possessed something of beauty, variously defined. "

Everett S. Allen

Intricate handiwork surrounds its artist.
FREDERICK D. ATWOOD

Swirls of fungi add a bizarre touch of beauty to a lush emerald carpet in Red Maple Swamp. LAURENCE PARENT

Dew drapes an ordinary caterpillar in diamonds. FREDERICK D. ATWOOD

Plump cranberries float to the surface for harvesting in Harwich, which hosts an annual cranberry harvest festival. WENDELL WELCH

When the first frost comes, the cranberry bogs begin to glow with burgundy red. There is a touch of dark purple in this color, too, so it suddenly looks as if some mythical giant had flung down his carpets to walk on.

Gladys Taber

The best berries bounce. JAMES LEMASS

One of three native fruits in North America, cranberries thrive in an ancient peat bog on Nantucket. PAUL REZENDES

Multicolored mums and a tumble of plump pumpkins announces autumn on the Cape. STEPHEN TRIMBLE

Color-starved gardeners seek out Eden's Flower Shop in Vineyard Haven. MICHAEL SHEDLOCK / NEW ENGLAND STOCK PHOTO

The merchandise at Farmer's Market can be simply stunning. ALISON SHAW

" Summer slides so gently into autumn on Cape Cod that it is easy to believe there will be no end. Day dreams toward twilight, skies are sapphire, the tide ebbs quietly. I begin to think time itself is arrested and the green leaves will stay forever on the trees. Gardens glow with color, with late roses and with carpets of zinnias and asters. "

Gladys Taber

Spring blooms on Main Street, Chatham, while its shops burst with enticing wares and its restaurants teem with delectable delights. SUSAN COLE KELLY

Fabric masterpieces are proudly displayed at a handicrafts fair at Drummer Boy Field in Brewster. JEFF GREENBERG

A leisurely stroll along artsy Commercial Street in Provincetown is an experience like no other. DAVID WEINTRAUB

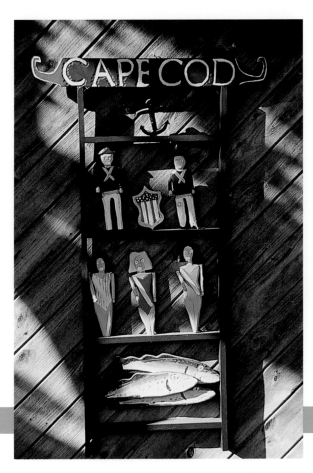

Artisans in Wellfleet craft the perfect Cape souvenirs. JEFF GREENBERG

❝ Cape Cod was always a place where you could find artsy-craftsy things... that you might be tempted to lug home. ❞

Charles N. Barnard

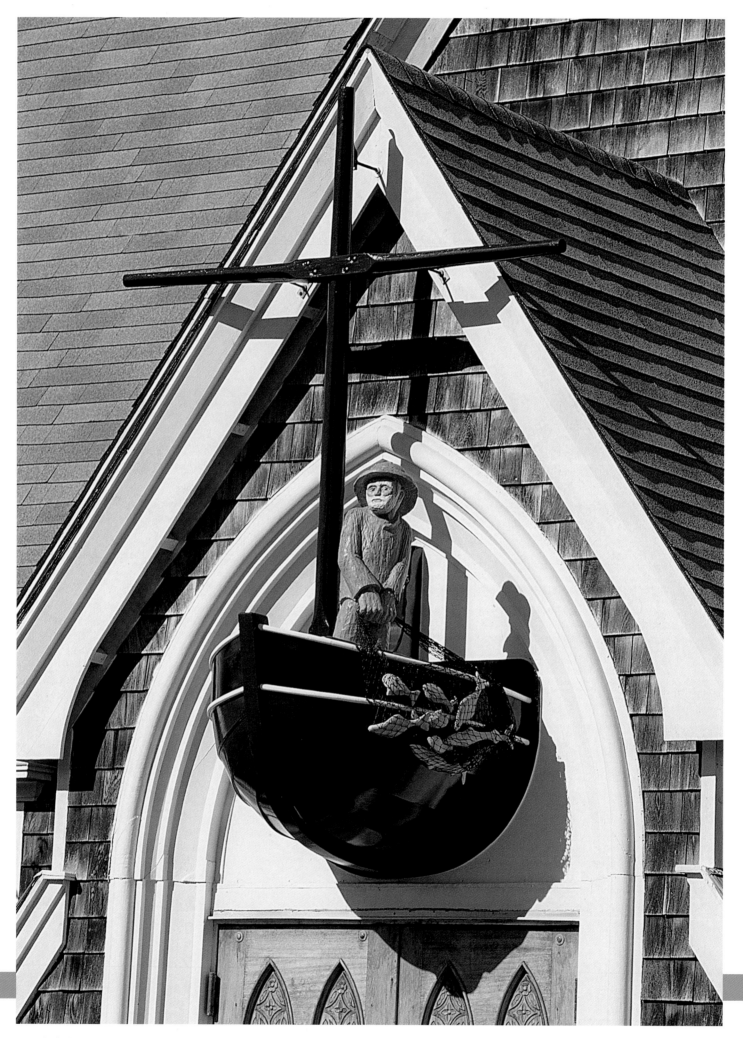

A tireless fisherman hauls in his catch at the entrance of St. Peter's Episcopal Church in Buzzards Bay. DAVID G. CURRAN

Rock-solid St. Barnabas Episcopal Church towers above downtown Falmouth. DAVID G. CURRAN

A unique work of art graces Our Lady of Lourdes
Catholic Church in Wellfleet. JEFF GREENBERG

Early morning sunlight highlights the fleet anchored on the glassy sea of Edgartown's Inner Harbor. PAUL REZENDES

𝗲 *The tempo of life on the Cape is, let us say frankly, slow. Nobody runs when they can walk. What doesn't get done one day may get done the next or the next.... Faces are etched by sea wind, browned by sun, but tension lines tend to disappear. The very immensity of the sea brings a sense of tranquillity.* 𝗳

Gladys Taber

Reflections on the seafaring life.   ALISON SHAW

Maritime mood. ALISON SHAW

The moon-tide laps gently against sailboats secure in their moorings at Provincetown Harbor.
WILLIAM JOHNSON / NEW ENGLAND STOCK PHOTO

A black skimmer's wings arch high in perfect symmetry. TOM VEZO

Calling it a day, a Steamship Authority ferry begins its return voyage to Woods Hole. ALISON SHAW

Highland Light, Cape Cod's oldest lighthouse, was moved back from the cliffs at Truro in 1996, when erosion threatened to sacrifice it to the sea. LAURENCE PARENT

Five active lighthouses warn mariners away from the coast known as the "Graveyard of the Atlantic." STEPHEN TRIMBLE

Nature's beam penetrates the lighthouse interior.
STEPHEN TRIMBLE

❝ A lighthouse has a certain mystery about it, I think. Perhaps this is because a man *lives inside, climbs the iron stairs to the blinding eye of the light itself, keeps faithful to his post in all kinds of weather, a sentinel of security in a dangerous world, the seaman's friend.* ❞

Charles N. Barnard

The Atlantic drums its tidal fingers on the beach at Newcomb Hollow. DAVID WEINTRAUB

66 *[A] man on the beach is a man nowhere; he can be claimed by neither land nor sea nor air, and such strange freedom changes his nature for so long as he stays between high-water mark and low. Let him walk ashore, and civilization has got him; let him put to sea, and the law is at his side; but on the beach he is as free as the gulls and the sandpipers.* 99

Henry C. Kittredge

A family enjoys a sunrise romp on the beach
KINDRA CLINEFF

Cool treats and warm smiles are a welcome sight to beach-goers on a sizzling summer day. JAMES LEMASS

" Summer people come from everywhere....
When you meet them on the beaches, they are
friendly, enthusiastic, full of the secure
happiness of parents who watch their little,
sunbrowned kids running around in the salt
air. Cape Cod, they always say, is such a
wonderful place. "

Charles N. Barnard

This treat passes the taste test. STEPHEN TRIMBLE

Sunseekers share Falmouth Heights Beach with weather-beaten turn-of-the-century homes. JAMES LEMASS

57

Beauty and the beachball. ALISON SHAW

Sailboarders bounce over the breakers off one of the area's nationally recognized windsurfing beaches.   DAVID G. CURRAN

A sinewy sailboarder tests his strength.
DAVID G. CURRAN

Unflagging southwesterly winds create a sailing mecca at Old Silver Beach in North Falmouth. JAMES LEMASS

> *When I detect a beauty in any of the recesses of nature, I am reminded, by the serene and retired spirit in which it requires to be contemplated, of the inexpressible privacy of life,—how silent and unambitious it is.*

Henry David Thoreau

Canada geese march in parade formation.
ALISON SHAW

More water than land, Lieutenant Island supports an extensive chain of marine life and a variety of land and sea birds. PAUL REZENDES

A boggle-eyed bullfrog patrols Barclay's Pond in Chatham. FREDERICK D. ATWOOD

The white water lily only blooms from dawn until noon. FREDERICK D. ATWOOD

Water lilies blanket the surface of Great Pond in the Beech Forest at Provincetown.   A.BLAKE GARDNER

Tenacious anglers set out to challenge their prey in Nauset Marsh. PAUL REZENDES

❝ Dawn unfolds gradually: first a decomposition of the dark and then a slow reassertion of forms. Day does not break, but unfurls in a steady gesture, opening from within. Clouds on the horizon fume and swell, and now the sun floats up out of the sea, shoots its red rays sideways, and disappears into a bank of clouds. ❞

Cynthia Huntington

The Railroad Bridge at Buzzards Bay has spanned the 480-foot-wide Cape Cod Canal since the early 1930s. PAUL REZENDES

> *Winter is not an easy season in New England—but without it, where would the ecstasy of a New England spring be?*

Gladys Taber

A male northern cardinal forages for food. TOM VEZO

Snow wraps Cape-stunted pines and scrub oaks in serene splendor. PAUL REZENDES

Beach grass anchors the snow-encrusted dunes of Chequesset Beach on windswept Great Island. A. BLAKE GARDNER

Cottonballs of snow make an agreeable frame for ice-locked Oyster Harbor at Woods Hole. DAVID G. CURRAN

Dry-docked boats are decked out for the holidays. DAVID G. CURRAN

Nantucket celebrates Yuletide at high tide. DAVID G. CURRAN

Depending on a ship's position, the stationary beam of Nobska Light glows red for dangerous waters or white for safe passage.   PAUL REZENDES

The 13-foot jawbones of a finback whale form the entrance to the Eastham Schoolhouse Museum. JEFF GNASS

In 1867, Wellfleet shipwrights built this French Second Empire home for a prosperous whaleboat captain, Edward Penniman.   LAURENCE PARENT

The Chatham Bars Inn, built as a hunting lodge in 1914, overlooks Pleasant Bay from an attractively landscaped bluff. JEFF GREENBERG

The John F. Kennedy Memorial in Hyannis pays a moving tribute to the town's most famous resident. THOMAS H. MITCHELL / NEW ENGLAND STOCK PHOTO

The Wauwinet Inn on Nantucket is nicknamed "The Ultimate" for its serene and romantic accommodations. ALISON FORBES / NEW ENGLAND STOCK PHOTO

Its quaint thatched roof and irresistible bargains attract hordes of shoppers to the Christmas Tree Shop near Sagamore. DAVID G. CURRAN

The Cape's oldest windmill was built in Plymouth in the 1600s and moved to Eastham in 1793.   JEFF GREENBERG

Built in 1797, the Old Grist Mill in Chatham required precise wind speeds of 20 to 25 miles an hour to operate. DAVID G. CURRAN

" *The most foreign and picturesque structures on the Cape, to an inlander...*
are the windmills,—gray-looking, octagonal towers, with long timbers slanting
to the ground in the rear, and there resting on a cartwheel, by which their fans
are turned round to face the wind... They looked loose and slightly locomotive,
like huge wounded birds, trailing a wing or a leg, and reminded one of
pictures of the Netherlands. "

Henry David Thoreau

The annual Wampanoag Powwow in Mashpee features three days of dancing, drumming, games, and a traditional clambake. DAVID G. CURRAN

The 30 tribes of the Wampanoag Nation lived harmoniously on the Cape for
centuries before the Pilgrims came ashore in 1620. DAVID G. CURRAN

In the summer, the harbors and marinas around the Cape bustle with people eager
to escape to the serenity of the sea. DAVID G. CURRAN

A Cape Codder enjoys being master of his fate and captain of his craft. ALISON SHAW

A crew pulls together during the Edgartown Regatta, one of the largest amateur
sailing events in the area. ALISON SHAW

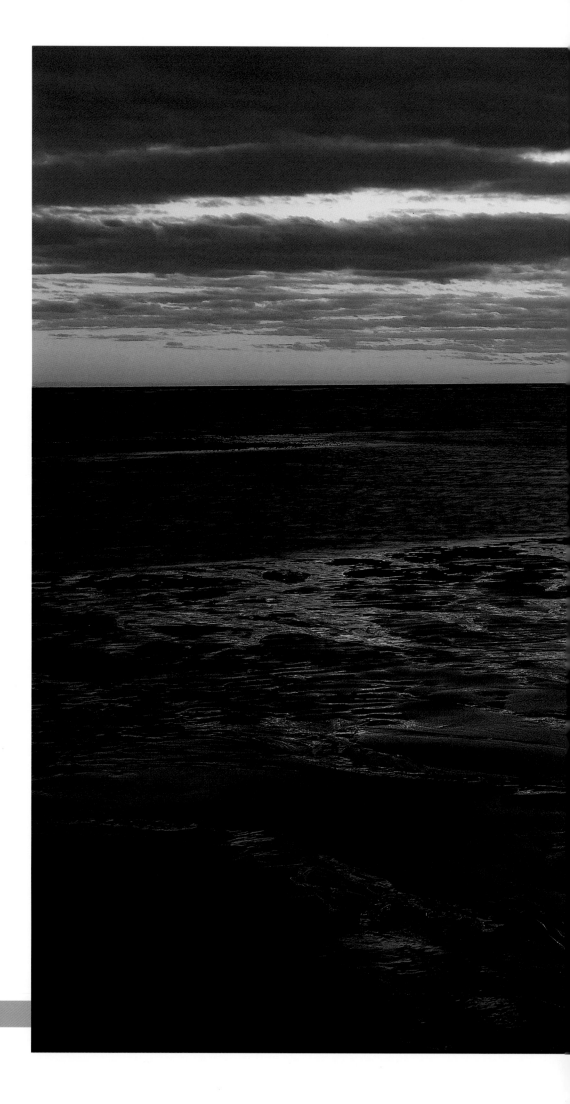

The three great elemental sounds in nature are the sound of rain, the sound of wind in a primeval wood, and the sound of outer ocean on a beach. I have heard them all, and of the three elemental voices, that of ocean is the most awesome, beautiful, and varied.... Listen to the surf, really lend it your ears, and you will hear in it a world of sounds: hollow boomings and heavy roarings, great watery tumblings and tramplings, long hissing seethes, sharp, rifle-shot reports, splashes, whispers, the grinding undertone of stones, and sometimes the vocal sounds that might be the half-heard talk of people in the sea.

Henry Beston

Sunsets over Cape Cod Bay, like this one seen from Great Island, can be particularly awe-inspiring. LAURENCE PARENT

Light and wave conspire to bring a "sea monster" to life. FREDERICK D. ATWOOD

66 *It is a confused pattern that the waves make in the open sea—a mixture of countless different wave trains, intermingling, overtaking, passing, or sometimes engulfing one another; each group differing from the others in the place and manner of its origin, in its speed, its direction of movement; some doomed never to reach any shore, others destined to roll across half an ocean before they dissolve in thunder on a distant beach.* 99

Rachel Carson

At low tide, the beach becomes a gallery for Atlantic artistry. R. HAMILTON SMITH

A sand sculpture survives the capricious nature of the sea. FREDERICK D. ATWOOD

The solitary tracks of a single bird compound a sense of wilderness. R. HAMILTON SMITH

Red foxes engage in a bit of nip and tuck. FREDERICK D. ATWOOD

*66 There is always
something poetic and
mysterious to me about these
tracks in the pits of the dunes;
they begin at nowhere,
sometimes with the faint
impression of an alighting
wing, and vanish as
suddenly into the trackless
nowhere of the sky. 99*

Henry Beston

Fox tracks punctuate the fragile beauty of the rolling dunes of the Province Lands. A. BLAKE GARDNER

In late summer, globular rose hips pop from beneath the magenta petals of a rugosa rose.   A. BLAKE GARDNER

The distinctive white buttonbush can withstand flooding. FREDERICK D. ATWOOD

Its fuzzy stamens inspired the common name of the moth mullein. FREDERICK D. ATWOOD

The roots of the chicory can be used to enrich coffee.
FREDERICK D. ATWOOD

The rare lady's slipper orchid blooms in early June.
FREDERICK D. ATWOOD

Placid water provides the perfect backdrop for quiet contemplation.   ALISON SHAW

A cheery porch invites conversation.   ALISON SHAW

A Chilmark beach house is shuttered with ocean blue.   ALISON SHAW

A campground cottage in Oak Bluffs welcomes a fresh breeze.   ALISON SHAW

" More distant, and strangely heroic, are those ones who sail out after the fish, whose lives are spent at sea, dragging offshore or fishing the dangerous ledges of Georges Bank. I see them beyond our window, heading out to sea where they crank up heavy nets in the cold, the water streaming through the mesh that strains with the bodies of fish. They go out by necessity, putting the same question to the sea over and over. Each time, the answer the sea gives is inarguable. "

Cynthia Huntington

The Old Harbor Life Saving Station, which is on the National Register of Historic Places, sheltered shipwreck victims in the 1880s. LAURENCE PARENT

A bicyclist glides across a boardwalk at Cape Cod National Seashore, breathing in the tart and salty smell of the sea. LAURENCE PARENT

" There was a pleasing secrecy in rowing this boat—or boating in general. It only seems like a conspicuous recreation; in fact, boating is a private passion... which may be why boat owners are independent, stubborn, finicky, and famous for doing exactly as they please. "

Paul Theroux

A sea kayaker embarks on a new adventure.
KINDRA CLINEFF

Nauset Marsh is one of the best locations for bird watching on the Cape, which has a reputation as a birder's paradise. DAVID WEINTRAUB

Ready oar not, here they come! JAMES LEMASS

A humpback puts on a whale of a show, thrilling the crowd that gathers to watch it. KINDRA CLINEFF

❝ Whales have been spouting offshore all week: finbacks playing in the waves, sometimes five or six of them together at once.... They swim to the surface, spout, and dive, showing a flash of fin or tail as they fold their enormous bulky selves back into the water; sometimes they seem to float on the surface, gently rolling over and back. ❞

Cynthia Huntington

The best time to see breaching humpback whales is in the spring or fall, when they migrate between feeding grounds. STEVEN MORELLO

Stellwagen Bank, about 8 miles northeast of Provincetown, is a favorite feeding ground for sea creatures great and small. FREDERICK D. ATWOOD

Some people never get the sand out of their hair. DAVID G. CURRAN

A toddler nets a discovery. ALISON SHAW

“ There are few things in life so rewarding as fishing. It offers the mystery of Christmas morning with unknown presents just out of sight beneath the tree or under the water's surface. It teaches patience, care with tools and pointy things and a gentleness towards life. It is an experience you can truly share with your child and a gift that they may value for the rest of their lives. ”

Michael Eichenseer

A lesson in casting is passed from generation to generation.   DAVID WEINTRAUB

The mighty tugboat, *Toot Toot*, takes a much-deserved rest in Falmouth Harbor.   JAMES LEMASS

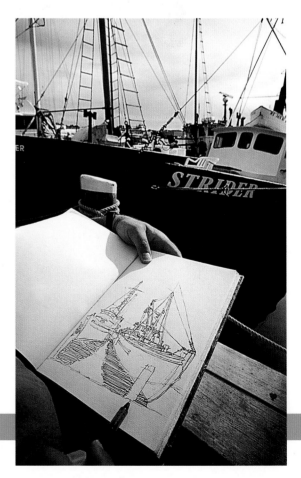

Artists often work outdoors at scenic spots throughout the Cape.   JEFF GREENBERG

A tugboat maneuvers a container barge through Cape Cod Canal, the world's widest sea-level canal. DAVID G. CURRAN

> *Tugboats may lack grace but they make it up in style, an unmistakable jauntiness. They are all muscle, little more than hulls and housing for big engines, snub-nosed and long-flanked.*
>
> Jan Adkins

Rowdy red and ready to row. ALISON SHAW

Adirondacks for four. ALISON SHAW

High and dry, a dinghy bides its time at Wellfleet. KINDRA CLINEFF

The Aquinnah Lighthouse on Gay Head, Martha's Vineyard, is eclipsed by the
dramatic red-clay cliffs of Aquinnah.   PAUL REZENDES

The quiet beaches of the Cape attract the federally threatened piping plover.   TOM VEZO

The sound of the surf is really the theme song of the Cape, for you hear it whether you are on Monument Road or Chickadee Lane or Barley Neck or Defiance Lane. Cape Codders need this reassurance that the sea is her own, still unconquered by man.

Gladys Taber

That's one spectacular water hazard on the seaside course at Chatham! KINDRA CLINEFF

" On some summer vacation or some country weekend we realize that what we are experiencing is more than merely a relief from the pressures of city life; that we have not merely escaped from something but also into something; that we have joined the greatest of all communities, which is not that of men alone but of everything that shares with us the great adventures of being alive. "

Joseph Wood Krutch

Championship and beginner-friendly links make the Cape a great golf destination. DAVID G. CURRAN

Most courses on the Cape, like Round Hill Public Golf Course in Sandwich, are open year-round. KINDRA CLINEFF

The Pilgrim Heights Trail meanders through woodland scented by rich, dank soil. PAUL REZENDES

A monarch rests on its namesake, butterflyweed. FREDERICK D. ATWOOD

Pitch pines invade a wild cranberry bog in the Province Lands of Truro.   PAUL REZENDES

This whitetail fawn is all ears and dewy eyes.   FREDERICK D. ATWOOD

they made it possible

Cape Cod on My Mind would have been impossible to produce without the keen eyes and technical skills of more than two dozen professional photographers. These women and men submitted their finest images, and the results show in this stunning collection of photos. What does not show is the work it took to get these images—the early mornings to capture the sunrise, the many hikes along sandy beaches, the endless hours of waiting for the perfect light, the hundreds of shots that didn't turn out quite right, and the level of technical skill that was acquired through years of experience and study. To all the photographers who contributed to *Cape Cod on My Mind*, we says thanks. We appreciate their art and their hard work.

The Publisher

Photographers in *Cape Cod on My Mind*

Frederick D. Atwood
Kindra Clineff
David G. Curran
A. Blake Gardner
Jeff Gnass
Jeff Greenberg
Susan Cole Kelly
James Lemass
Steven Morello
Laurence Parent
Paul Rezendes
Alison Shaw
R. Hamilton Smith
Stephen Trimble
Tom Vezo
David Weintraub
Wendell Welch

New England Stock Photo
  Thomas P. Benincas, Jr.
  Alison Forbes
  William Johnson
  Thomas H. Mitchell
  Lou Palmieri
  Frank Siteman
  Michael Shedlock

© 2000 by Falcon® Publishing, Inc.
Helena, Montana

All rights reserved, including the right to reproduce any part of this book in any form, except brief quotations for reviews, without the written permission of the publisher.

Design, typesetting, and other prepress work by Falcon Publishing, Inc., Helena, Montana. Printed in Korea.

Library of Congress Number: 00-131347

ISBN 1-56044-787-7

For extra copies of this book please check with your local bookstore, or write Falcon®, P.O. Box 1718, Helena, MT 59624, or call toll-free 1-800-582-2665.
Visit our web site at www.FalconBooks.com.

Front cover photos:
  Brant Point Lighthouse, Nantucket PAUL REZENDES
  Lobster dinner ALISON SHAW
Back cover photos:
  Vineyard Haven Harbor, Martha's Vineyard
    PAUL REZENDES
  Old Harbor Life Saving Station JEFF GNASS
  Nature's bounty, Dennis STEPHEN TRIMBLE
  Striped bass, Chatham fishing pier KINDRA CLINEFF
End papers: STEPHEN TRIMBLE
Design and layout: LAURIE GIGETTE GOULD
Series editor: GAYLE SHIRLEY
Text research: CHERYL HUBAN

acknowledgments

The publisher gratefully acknowledges the following sources from which the quotations used in this book were taken:

Front flap, title page, and pages 14, 29, 40, 43, 48, 66, and 105 from *My Own Cape Cod*, by Gladys Taber. Philadelphia and New York: J. B. Lippincott Company, 1971.

Pages 3, 10, 82, and 86 from *The Outermost House*, by Henry Beston. New York: Viking Press, 1971. Originally published in 1928.

Pages 6 and 55 from *Mooncussers of Cape Cod*, by Henry C. Kittredge. Boston and New York: Houghton Mifflin, 1937.

Pages 9 and 77 from *Cape Cod*, by Henry David Thoreau. New York: Bramhall House, 1951. Originally published in 1865.

Page 12 from *Coast to Coast*, by James Morris. London: Faber, 1956.

Page 18 from *Cape Cod Architecture*, by Clair Baisly. Yarmouthport, MA: Parnassus Imprints, 1989.

Pages 23 and 84 from *The Sea Around Us*, by Rachel Carson. New York: Oxford University Press, 1951.

Pages 31, 64, 92, and 96 from *The Salt House: A Summer on the Dunes of Cape Cod*, by Cynthia Huntington. Hanover and London: University Press of New England, 1999.

Page 36 from *The Sense of Wonder*, by Rachel Carson. New York: Harper & Row, 1956.

Page 38 from *This Quiet Place: A Cape Cod Chronicle*, by Everett S. Allen. Boston and Toronto: Little, Brown and Company, 1971.

Pages 45, 53, 56, and 112 from *The Winter People: A Return to Cape Cod*, by Charles N. Barnard. New York: Dodd, Mead & Company, 1973.

Page 60 from *The Natural History Essays*, by Henry David Thoreau. Salt Lake City: Peregrine Smith Books, 1989.

Page 80 from *Homes in the Wilderness: A Pilgrim's Journal of Plymouth Plantation in 1620*, by William Bradford and others of the Mayflower company, ed. by Margaret Wise Brown. Hamden, CT: Linnet Books, 1988.

Page 94 from *Sunrise with Monsters*, by Paul Theroux. Boston: Houghton Mifflin, 1985.

Page 98 from "Fishing with Your Kids Is Easy," Cape Cod Outdoors™ website, www.capecodoutdoors.com

Page 101 from *Workboats*, by Jan Adkins. New York: Charles Scribner's Sons, 1985.

Page 106 from *The Best Nature Writing of Joseph Wood Krutch*, by Joseph Wood Krutch. New York: William Morrow, 1969.

A sailboat catches the last gleam of day in Menemsha Harbor on Martha's Vineyard.

❝ It was a theater for sunsets, a promontory especially dredged up from the ocean bottom from which to view the end of a summer's day. The great, fiery disc of the sun would slip beneath the rim of the sea, turning molten red, lighting the sky and the water and the sands first with ember-hot reflections, then with delicate pastel afterglow. ❞

Charles N. Barnard